W9-BYF-718

Air Devils

Sky Racers, Sky Divers, and Stunt Pilots

by Ellen Hopkins

Perfection Learning® Corporation

Inside Illustrations: Michael A. Aspengren
Book Design: Kay Ewald

Image Credits: AFP/Corbis p. 14 (bottom); Bettmann/Corbis pp. 26 (bottom),
41 (bottom), 45 (top); Corbis p. 50 (bottom); Brent Finley p. 15; Museum of
Flight/Corbis pp. 33 (bottom), 39 (bottom); National Air and Space Museum,
Smithsonian Institution pp. 34, 40 (top), 43; Tim Wagner p. 19

Ed Anderson p. 53; Art Today pp. 6, 7, 8, 10, 11, 12, 14 (top), 16, 17, 20,
21, 22, 23, 24 (middle, bottom), 26 (top), 30 (bottom), 32 (bottom), 37, 40
(middle), 42 (top), 46 (top, bottom), 49 (top); Mark A. Chronister p. 58;
Digital Stock pp. 47 (bottom), 48 (top, bottom), 49 (bottom), 51 (top,
bottom), 52; John H. Garrett pp. 55, 61; Rolf J. Hancock p. 57; Dick Hill
p. 4 (inset); John Hopkins pp. 54 (bottom), 56; John L. Jenkins p. 54 (top);
Library of Congress pp. 3, 24 (top), 25 (bottom), 27, 29, 30 (top), 31
(bottom), 33 (top), 36, 38 (bottom); Jack McFall p. 5 (bottom); Lorain M.
Miller pp. 4, 5 (top), 64; National Archives p. 25 (top), 30 (middle), 31 (top),
32 (top), 41 (top), 46 (middle), 47 (top), 48 (middle), 49 (middle), 50 (top);
NOAA p. 40 (bottom); United States Air Force pp. 38 (top), 39 (top), 42
(bottom), 44, 45 (bottom), 51 (middle); United States Navy p. 50 (middle)

Dedication

To my family, who believed in me.

About the Author

Ellen Hopkins lives with her family, four dogs, two cats, and
three tanks of fish near Carson City, Nevada. A California native,
Ellen moved to the Sierra Nevada to ski. While writing for a Lake
Tahoe newspaper, she discovered many exciting things and
fascinating people. This book is about some of them. Ellen hopes it
leads her readers to reach for their dreams.

Acknowledgment

With special thanks to Jim Bozarth,
Patti Johnson, Jon Sharp, and David Price.

Text © 2000 by Perfection Learning® Corporation.
All rights reserved. No part of this book may be used or reproduced in
any manner whatsoever without written permission from the publisher.
Printed in the United States of America. For information, contact
Perfection Learning® Corporation, 1000 North Second Avenue,
P.O. Box 500, Logan, Iowa 51546-0500.
Phone: 1-800-831-4190 • Fax: 1-712-644-2392
Paperback ISBN 0-7891-5146-4
Cover Craft® ISBN 0-7807-9308-0
7 8 9 10 11 12 PP 12 11 10 09 08 07

AEROPLANE, "RED WING," HAMMONDSPORT, N.Y.
FIRST AMERICAN PUBLIC FLIGHT, MAR. 12, 1908

Table of Contents

Introduction
The Air Devils

You hear them before you see them. The low buzz blooms as it nears. Soon it becomes an angry growl.

Suddenly, eight tiny planes pop into view. Side by side, the souped-up **crop dusters** dash down the runway. Wing to wing, they lift off and climb into the desert sky.

The loudspeaker booms. "Ladies and gentlemen, you have a race!"

At first, they fly tight like noisy geese. Tall poles on the ground called *pylons* mark the course. Around them the planes zoom. They get as close as they dare. Cutting in front adds penalty seconds. But swinging wide costs too. Soon the fastest pull away.

Out comes the white flag. One lap to go. It's time for risky moves. Down the back stretch, the second-place airplane climbs. Then he dives past the leader to take the checkered flag. The crowd goes crazy as the winner wags his wings in a victory salute.

Biplane rounds pylon

4

Welcome to today's air racing, the most exciting and fastest motor sport on earth. These smaller planes race at Indy-car speeds.

Unlimited "Sneak Attack"

But the big boys, the **unlimited** racers, roar down the straightaways twice as fast. That's over 500 mph. All the while, they fight wind, air currents, and gravity. Winning takes speed, skill, and spunk.

There's more. The all-American show starts with the national anthem. But you have to look way up to find the flag. It's carried by a skydiving team, leaving trails of red, white, and blue smoke.

Between races, a different breed of flier takes to the air. In **biplanes**, big planes, or jets, these **aerial** acrobats flip, dive and loop, fly upside down, and race dragsters. They are stunt pilots, sky divers, and sky racers. What a party!

So climb aboard. Fly with the air devils. Take a ride you'll never forget.

Unlimiteds

Racing for the Sky

Do you like games or contests? Do you enjoy sports or races? Did you ever bet you could do something? Then did you *have* to prove it?

Well, you're not alone. Most people like to compete. And everyone wants to win. It's human nature.

Hop into the Way-Back Machine. Rewind time a million years. See that caveman over there? He's that hairy guy carving a spear. Let's call him Mr. C. For him, competition was anything but fun.

Could Mr. C bag a deer? Or would a tiger bag Mr. C? Was Mr. C stronger than another caveman who wanted the same deer? Could either outrun a prairie fire or outswim a swift river? To Mr. C and his family, winning often meant staying alive.

Now roll forward several centuries. As people found safety in numbers, families gathered to form **tribes**.

These groups often wandered. They settled where food was plentiful. If two tribes wanted the same land, they competed. Winning was about keeping property—or losing it.

Tribes needed leaders. Those with the most know-how took charge.

Contests proved skill. Before machines, contests were simple. Who could run fastest or jump longest? Who could throw farthest or aim straightest? Who was best?

Then people found better ways of doing things. Each new invention brought a new challenge. Would a bicycle beat a buggy? Could a horse outrun a train or a Model T car? Which engine was faster, gas or steam? Which was better?

Deciding "better or best" made for exciting competitions. But few offered the thrills and chills of contests in the sky.

But first someone had to figure out how to reach that dangerous new frontier. Who would lead the way?

Early on, people dreamed of flying. Remember our caveman? Mr. C probably watched birds with envy. Plodding across the land was hard work. Soaring like an eagle was the way to go! It looked so easy. Not to mention it also looked like fun. All you needed were wings. Right?

During the **Dark Ages** (400 A.D. to 1000 A.D.), a few brave—or crazy—souls made wings of feathers and wax. Then they jumped off cliffs or towers. But no matter how hard they flapped their arms, they couldn't soar like eagles. They crashed like boulders!

So they plotted on paper, drawing fancy **ornithopters**. These "bird machines" had giant wings. But different things like springs made them flap. A few people built these machines. But they never got off the ground.

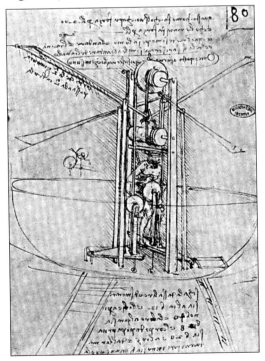

Artist and inventor Leonardo da Vinci studied birds for 40 years. "Write of swimming underwater," he said, "and you will have the flight of the bird through the air."

As Christopher Columbus sailed for the New World, da Vinci sketched flying machines. He drew 150 in all. Many looked like today's helicopters.

Da Vinci's ornithopter design

Da Vinci never tried to build his flying machines. He knew the proper power source did not exist then. He also designed a "tent made of linen" that might have worked like a parachute. But he never built it either.

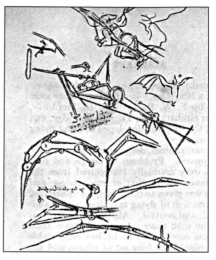

When da Vinci died in 1519, his sketchbooks went to a friend. These lay forgotten for over 300 years. Had they turned up sooner, humans could have taken a shortcut on their long journey to the sky.

People had the means to fly long before they did. The clues were everywhere. Campfire smoke drifted skyward since it was lighter than air. Boomerangs and feathered arrows showed how air pressure against wing surfaces created **lift**. The blades of ancient Roman windmills acted like propellers.

The kite was invented 2,000 years ago in China. It made manned flight possible. It's not such a big leap from kite to glider. All it took was the vision to harness the forces of nature and the courage to do it.

Even today the sky holds mystery and danger. Long ago, it held magic. There were flying carpets and chariots, winged horses and dragons, and angels and gods. Legends like those of **Daedalus and Icarus** warned of challenging the heavens. No wonder few people tried to capture smoke in fabric or hang beneath giant kites.

But a handful did. Their curiosity and imagination made the age-old dream of flying come true.

Chapter 2

Soaring to New Heights

Try this. Snap a small balloon over the top of an empty soda bottle. It hangs limp. Now set the bottle into a pan of hot water. See how it slowly starts to **inflate**. This happens because the hot water heats the bottle and warms the air inside.

Hot air is lighter than cold air, so it rises and fills the balloon. That is also why smoke, which is heated air, drifts upward.

We don't know who first figured that out. But people may have ballooned a very long time ago.

Strange ruins mark the plains near Nazca, Peru. Experts think they were an irrigation system built before 1200 A.D. To construct the mazelike design, someone high up had to give directions. Did ancient Indians balloon?

In 1975, a group of scientists decided to see if it was possible. They made a balloon of fabric available in Peru 1,000 years ago. Then they filled it with smoke from a fire pit. The manned balloon rose 400 feet and stayed in the air for three minutes.

Jim Winker helped with the project. He believes early Peruvian Indians might have been the first **aeronauts**. "There may be other explanations for the Nazca markings," he said. "But this is certainly the best one I have heard."

9

In August 1709, a priest stood before the king of Portugal. Father de Gusmao had just returned from the jungles of Peru. He swore he'd watched the natives take to the air in smoke-filled balloons. From above, they tracked game and the movement of enemy tribes. The king wanted proof.

Gusmao built a basic balloon of bark and canvas. Using a number of **spirits**, he lit a flame beneath the balloon. Heated air filled the fabric. His Majesty's court "oohed" and "aahed" as it drifted toward the ceiling.

Then the bark caught fire. The balloon crashed and whoosh! went the royal tapestries. The king was too numb to care. Maybe people really could fly!

Imaginations soared. Around the world, the race to **ascend** began. While some experimented with **hydrogen**, others kept at the hot-air idea. The French Montgolfier brothers won the first **"heat"** in 1783.

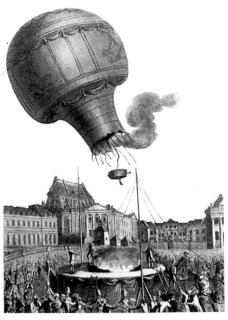

It was a late summer day. In Versailles, around 30,000 people had gathered at the palace. King Louis XVI gave the signal. The Montgolfiers' hot-air balloon rose two miles high. But it was **tethered**.

A sheep, a duck, and a rooster rode in its wicker basket. After eight minutes, the balloon leaked air and crashed. The animals weren't hurt. Although the sheep did step on the rooster.

The stunt did not impress the king. Flight as transportation? Highly unlikely! But he did allow the experiments to continue.

A few months later, two men lifted off from Paris in a hot-air balloon. Some 400,000 people came to watch. It was the largest gathering of people in the world up to that time.

They watched the balloon drift across the city. It went 3,000 feet in 25 minutes.

Ten days later, professor J. A. C. Charles launched the first manned hydrogen balloon. Before long, aeronauts ascended all across Europe.

In America, the first person to balloon was 13-year-old Edward Warren. It seems the gentleman who built the balloon didn't have the nerve to fly it. "How splendid," he said, "to find such a brave volunteer." In June 1784, the daring lad rose above a large Boston crowd in a tethered balloon.

The first free-flight balloon in the United States wouldn't happen for almost ten years.

People were in the air. Now they wanted to go somewhere. In 1785, Vincent Lunardi ballooned from London to Ware. He traveled 24 miles in only 2½ hours. With him went a pigeon (which flew off), a cat (which ran away on touchdown), and a dog (whose loyalty was tested). The saucy Italian became the toast of England.

One of his fans was an actress of the day. She asked to go for a ride. Lunardi said yes without setting eyes on her. But he'd heard she was stunning.

Letitia Ann Sage proved to be not only beautiful but very large. She took up most of the basket. Lunardi had to give up his own seat.

Vincent Lunardi

Letitia and a Mr. Biggin, another paying passenger, lifted off without a pilot. They landed in a field. The only danger was from the farmer whose beans they had squashed. The actress soothed the man with her famous smile. Then she went to town for a big supper. Flying had made her hungry and "better pleased than with any other event in my life," she said.

There was really no need for a pilot. Lunardi himself could do little to control the balloon. The wind decided which way they'd go, how long they'd stay up, and where they'd come down. This problem made flying chancy for even the best aeronaut. Who wanted to land in a swamp or face a farmer's pitchfork?

New competitions arose anyway. How high could a balloon go? How far and how fast? How long could it stay aloft? Could

it cross mountains or seas? Were there aeronauts brave enough to find out? The first to try such a terrifying voyage was French pilot Jean-Pierre (J. P.) Blanchard.

Blanchard was a born showman. He loved drama. In 1785, few things could offer the drama of crossing the English Channel by air. This dangerous stretch of sea separates England and France.

Blanchard decided to give it a go. American John Jeffries rode shotgun. They lifted off from Dover. All went well at first. A gentle breeze carried them toward France. Sailors and fishermen shouted and pointed. They'd never seen such a thing!

Halfway across, however, the wind picked up. It tossed the balloon too high. Blanchard released hydrogen. But more than he should have. The balloon fell toward rough seas.

"Quick!" he shouted. "We must shed weight!"

The sandbags went first. Then the food went. Still the balloon sank. They tossed out the anchors, the oars, and an experimental propeller. But still they went down. They were even closer to the water.

Overboard went overcoats, hats, and shoes. Blanchard even threw away his trousers. The balloon lifted a little.

Shivering with cold, the men finally reached the other side. A tall stand of trees loomed. The balloon bounced through the treetops until Blanchard spotted a clearing. Somehow they landed safely.

In order for aeronauts to win distance contests, they knew they must understand the wind. Trial and error taught them that airflows change at different **altitudes**. Simply going higher or lower could change a balloon's speed or direction.

In the 1830s, American John Wise used balloons to study weather. As he rose higher and higher, he found long, swift currents of air. He had discovered **jet streams**. Now balloonists could journey across oceans and continents.

Other problems surfaced. As you rise, air becomes colder and thinner. Without oxygen, balloonists could only go up so far if they wanted to keep breathing. But how far? they wondered.

In 1862, two Englishmen soared to 36,000 feet without oxygen. Yet a few years later, three French balloonists blacked out at 25,000 feet. Only one came back alive. With portable oxygen and better equipment, pilots now touch the heavens.

In 1931, a Swiss scientist fastened an airtight **gondola** to a big balloon. Auguste Piccard rose ten miles high. He was the first person to reach the **stratosphere**.

Three years later, Piccard's twin brother, Jean-Felix, ascended 11 miles. Then in 1961, two United States Navy officers rose 113,500 feet to set the current world record.

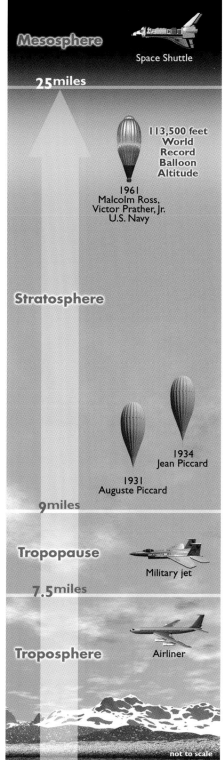

Mesosphere

Space Shuttle

25miles

113,500 feet
World
Record
Balloon
Altitude
1961
Malcolm Ross,
Victor Prather, Jr.
U.S. Navy

Stratosphere

1934
Jean Piccard

1931
Auguste Piccard

9miles

Tropopause

Military jet

7.5miles

Troposphere

Airliner

not to scale

Modern balloon competitions are mostly just fun. There are all different kinds. In cross-country and spot-landing contests, pilots must take off and land within a set amount of time. The cross-country winner travels farthest. The spot-landing champ touches down closest to a certain point.

Other balloonists play a game called "Hare and Hounds." The "hare" balloon takes off five or ten minutes ahead of the "hounds." It drifts with the wind, changing altitude from time to time to throw the chase balloons off track. When he lands, the others follow. The one that touches down closest to the hare wins. The game takes skill, but it also takes luck. As always, the wind often decides the winner.

Before 1999, one serious goal remained. No one had circled the globe nonstop. Balloonists called the quest the "last great adventure." Failed attempts numbered 19. Sometimes weather was to blame. Sometimes a country wouldn't let foreign pilots use its **airspace**.

On March 1, 1999, Bertrand Piccard and Brian Jones lifted off from the snowy Swiss Alps. Bertrand, Auguste Piccard's grandson, had tried the trip twice before. This time he made it.

At times, the men rode the jet stream at 100 mph. The 26,600-mile journey took 478 hours. Piccard thanked "the invisible hand" that guided them over Africa, India, Asia, and across the Pacific.

East of Central America, the 180-foot-high balloon stalled. The men were trapped seven miles high in the icy cold sky. Piccard and

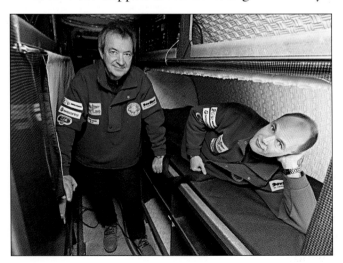

Jones could barely breathe. Then Orbiter 3 caught the jet stream again. It rocketed across the Atlantic and touched down in Egypt on March 21.

"We are having great difficulty realizing our dreams have come true," said Piccard. "We are with the angels."

Brian Jones (left) and Bertrand Piccard (right) in the gondola of their balloon

Chapter **3**

Wings of Silk

If you like the X games on TV, you've probably seen sky surfing. It's part skydiving, part gymnastics.

A two-person team jumps from a plane at 13,000 feet. One has a helmet-mounted camera. The other "surfs" on a sky board. It looks like a short snowboard. Down the team falls at about 120 mph.

The camera shoots video. The judges on the ground are too far away to see what's going on. They'll watch the tape and give the surfer points for difficulty, creativity, and control. The

camera work counts too. It can account for up to half the score.

The surfer begins a routine. There are flips, spins, and tumbles. The surfer does a headstand and "helicopters." After 60 seconds, *zip* go the rip cords. The pair parachutes gracefully to the ground.

Amy Baylie-Haas skydives and pilots for United Parcel Service. She, unlike most women, also sky surfs. But Amy loves the challenge. She calls the sport "awesome . . . It's like playing in the softest playground there is—the sky!"

Awesome to be sure! Even in this age of **supersonic** flight and space shuttles, sky surfing makes you go "wow!" There are no motors, no cockpits, no controls. There's just a person with a wing of silk, riding the wind.

Now pretend you lived more than 200 years ago. In that age of **superstition**, you've never seen a train (first built in 1804). You've never heard of a bicycle (1818), let alone an automobile (1886).

Imagine looking up. Someone's falling from the sky. Well, not exactly falling. He's attached to a piece of fabric that slows his **descent**. Down he drops, swinging back and forth. He hits the ground and walks away!

Now *that* was awesome. No wonder huge crowds flocked to parachute drops.

In 1785, J. P. Blanchard designed a parachute that could help steer a balloon. He toyed with his invention, tying the canvas to a small basket and dropping it. How slowly it floated to earth! Would it work with weight inside?

Blanchard tried it with a dog. The animal touched down safely. Blanchard had a hit. He went on tour. He parachuted dogs and cats all over Europe and America. Oddly, he never thought to design a chute that could break a person's fall.

But another Frenchman did. Andre Garnerin was a soldier. Taken prisoner in Austria, he dreamed of escape for three long years. He'd heard about Blanchard's parachute. Might a bigger one carry a man off a prison wall and across the river to freedom?

Garnerin went free before he could find out. Back home in France, he constructed the parachute anyway.

In October 1797, he took it for a test dive. News of the man's crazy plan spread across Paris. Thousands turned out to watch. Most thought he'd kill himself. He surprised them.

Lifted into the air by a balloon, Garnerin rose 6,000 feet. Then he cut the parachute loose for the ten-minute ride of a

lifetime. Down he drifted, enjoying every second until the wild sway made him sick. The last thing he remembered was hitting the ground hard.

It was back to the drawing board. New and improved parachutes followed.

In 1815, Garnerin talked his niece, Eliza, into trying a drop. She loved it and went up every chance she got. Soon she could do tricks in the air. A new competition was born—**aerobatics**.

Eliza toured Europe between 1816 and 1836. Each time, she did harder and harder stunts. People paid dearly to watch a pretty young lady somersault through the air. Other parachutists followed her lead. For the next 75 years, "soaring and chuting" was all the rage.

By the end of the 1800s, London's Alexandra Palace was a happening place. "Ally Pally" had a boating lake and a racecourse. There were grounds for carnivals, parades, and fireworks displays. One of Ally Pally's great showmen, Auguste Gaudron, led a team of parachute stunt jumpers.

Another showman was Texan Sam Cody. He thrilled crowds with his Wild West show. His wife was the star attraction. Lela Cody stood stock-still while a blindfolded Sam shot an egg from her head. One night he missed. A slug grazed her scalp. Lela ended her career before another bullet did.

Eighteen-year-old Dolly Shepherd volunteered to fill in. She almost changed her mind when the pistol pointed her way. Instead, she closed her eyes tight. Cody's aim was true that night. Eighty years later, Dolly wrote that the experience "opened the door to adventures beyond my wildest dreams."

Gaudron rewarded the teen with a tour of his balloon **emporium**. The parachutes grabbed her attention.

"Would you like to try a jump?" Gaudron asked.

Dolly surprised him. "Yes!" she exclaimed.

Her training lasted exactly 30 minutes. Decked in navy knickers and tall boots, Dolly climbed into Gaudron's balloon. At 2,000 feet, he said simply, "Get ready . . . there's a nice, green field over there
. . . Remember how to land . . . GO!"

Dolly called her first fall a mixture of fright and delight. She landed perfectly, grinning from ear to ear. Gaudron asked her to join his team as the "Parachute Queen." Audiences loved her good looks. Often she strutted among them and discussed the wonder of the wide, blue yonder.

Like most skydivers, Dolly had many close calls, landing in trees or on rooftops. Once her parachute came loose from the harness. She tumbled into the crowd. Several large women cushioned her fall.

Another time, her friend's parachute jammed. Dolly jumped close enough for her to grab hold and ride safely to the ground. It was history's first midair rescue.

One day, Dolly imagined she heard a voice. "Don't come up again or you'll be killed." Her navy knickers went into the rag bag. At 25, she wanted to live a long, full life. Her balloon career ended. She'd had plenty of adventure.

Stunt jumpers are still an adventurous lot. Ask Jim Bozarth, a pro stuntman with over 1,000 jumps under his belt. You may have seen him skydive in movies like *Honeymoon in Vegas* or *Red Dawn*. "Jumpers are the freest of spirits," explained Jim. "You may never find anyone more free."

Jim said you don't have to be a daredevil to skydive. But it does help. "One time I was jumping with the Into the Fire skydiving team. We were opening the big hot-air balloon festival in New Mexico. Local air traffic delayed our start time. Finally, we got the go-ahead. Six of us jumped, did our free fall, then opened our parachutes.

"We had no idea the balloons had already launched. There were dozens in the air. We had to fly over, under, and around them. All of us cleared the maze and landed safely, if a bit frazzled."

Modern equipment has made the sport safer, but not risk-free. Jim was badly hurt in 1996. He was performing on a team jump with the Flying Elvises. Doctors told him he might never walk again. Let alone skydive. But Jim fought back. It took a year of hard work to get strong. All he could think about was jumping.

"I did consider quitting. My wife sure wanted me to. But I'm one of the lucky people who has found his place in life. Quit? Naaaaaaaaaaaaaa!"

The words of a true air devil.

Chapter 4

Canvas, Wire, and Wood

As Dolly Shepherd wowed Ally Pally crowds, a new competition began. Balloons had given people their first taste of flight. But to really go places, an airship needed power. It needed a motor. **Dirigibles** were chancy. Hydrogen caught fire easily. Engines sparked. Putting them together could—and did—lead to disaster.

Powered kites looked like the way to go. On both sides of the Atlantic, the race to fly an **aeroplane** hit its stride.

In Kitty Hawk, North Carolina, Orville and Wilbur Wright crossed the finish line first. On December 17, 1903, these two American bicycle makers stood on a windy beach. Their *Flyer* rested on a wooden track. The fabric and wire machine didn't have tires. But it did have a motor.

Orville lay flat on the lower wing. He brought the engine up to full power. *Flyer* slid along the track, picking up speed. Wilbur ran alongside to steady the aeroplane.

A dirigible is a powered balloon. It is capable of being steered. The first dirigibles were filled with hydrogen gas. This gas proved to be too explosive. Now dirigibles, such as the Fuji Film and Goodyear blimps, are filled with helium.

Orville Wright flies 120 feet on December 17, 1903.

At 10:35, *Flyer* lifted into the air. A single photo recorded the 12-second flight. The aeroplane had taken off!

It was a giant leap. So why didn't the world seem to care? News traveled slowly in 1903. It took months for people to hear about *Flyer*. Many didn't believe it. Others couldn't see what it meant. Who wanted to fly? Those new automobiles were scary enough. At least if you crashed a motorcar, you might walk away.

But the Wrights knew Planet Earth had just grown smaller. Trips that once took weeks would take only hours. Freight and passengers would arrive safe and sound.

Yes, *Flyer* had a few problems. You couldn't really steer it. And the pilot couldn't see where he was going. These were minor design flaws. But easily fixed.

The brothers got busy. Two years later, they'd worked out the bugs. Their remodeled *Flyer* could turn, bank, do figure eights, and fly cross-country. In 1908, Orville made history's first hour-long flight.

By then, others were in the air.

Orville (left) and Wilbur (right) Wright

Each tried to improve the Wright biplane design. In France, the Voison brothers added a larger tail. This made the plane more stable.

At the same time, Louis Bleriot built single-wing machines. These lighter **monoplanes** were easier to **maneuver**.

In England, Sam Cody dazzled people again. This time in a biplane. In true Wild West style, Cody achieved the first powered takeoff from British soil.

Glenn Curtiss

Back in the United States, motorcycle racer Glen Curtiss created a light but powerful engine. He offered it to the Wrights. But they turned it down. They had their own "bigger, better" motor. So Curtiss went to the Aerial Experimentation Association (AEA). Together they built a series of planes called "dromes."

This fierce rivalry led to a steady stream of improvements. Each made airplanes safer. More horsepower made them faster. Better fuel systems let them go farther.

Beyond the machinery, pilots learned how to fly. Ordinary people could then climb aboard. But how could they prove that flying was safe? The answer was competitions!

On July 4, 1908, a large crowd gathered at Hammondsport, New York. Families picnicked. Reporters wrote in notebooks. Photographers polished lenses. A motion picture crew stood waiting. They had all heard about airplanes. But few had seen one.

Would Glen Curtiss' *June Bug* win the *Scientific American* trophy? The magazine had offered $12,500 to the pilot who could fly over a mile.

Wind and rain delayed things. People began to wonder. Was this just a hoax?

Glenn Curtiss

Glenn Curtiss and *June Bug*, July 4, 1908

But late in the day, out rolled *June Bug*. The motor sputtered then caught. Down the runway the plane taxied, faster and faster. Suddenly, it lifted off—20 feet high and trailing smoke. Curtiss landed short on his first try. But he went well over a mile on the second. America had seen its first aerial event.

A month later, Wilbur Wright arrived at Le Mans raceway in France. The American amazed French spectators with his skill. But his passenger surprised them more.

Edith Berg didn't look like a daredevil. She looked like a schoolteacher. Her husband was the Wrights' business manager. Hart O. Berg knew his stuff. To please an audience, give 'em something new. A woman in the air would surely do.

Wilbur Wright

Edith tied her long skirts around her knees and climbed aboard the two-seater *Flyer*. Delight showed ear to ear. Wilbur got in beside her. His mechanics started the motor. Then they unhooked the anchor wire.

Flyer shot straight up five stories high. Edith's stomach flip-flopped. Her smile grew even wider. She was the first woman to ride in an airplane. And she thought the two-minute flight was much too short!

Back home in September, Orville Wright took his newest two-seater to Fort Myer, Virginia. There he stunned Army officials with a series of perfect test flights. Each time he went up, he flew farther.

Body taken from September 17, 1908, crash of Orville Wright's biplane

But on the last day, the plane's propeller cracked. The biplane crashed. Orville was badly hurt. His passenger died and became the first person to lose his life in an airplane. Orville returned to the air in less than a year. In October 1909, he set an altitude record of 1,000 feet.

That was a banner year for aviation. Pilots took off in Canada and all across Europe. A million New Yorkers first glimpsed an airplane when Wilbur Wright flew up the Hudson River.

In France, Louis Bleriot and Hubert Latham raced to cross the English Channel. Bleriot won. He flew the 20-mile flight in 37 minutes.

Hubert Latham

The highlight of 1909 was the world's first air meet. It was held at Reims, France. What an exciting week! A quarter of a million people turned out, including most of Europe's royalty. Wet August weather couldn't dampen their spirits. Soggy fields couldn't keep record after record from falling.

Reims, France—1909. Henri Farman wins. **24**

Henri Farman won the distance prize with a flight of 112 miles in three hours. Hubert Latham claimed the altitude trophy with a height of 508 feet.

Glenn Curtiss was the only American there. He set the speed record of 47.65 mph. Louis Bleriot might have edged him out. But his gas tank caught fire and blew up. Though badly burned, he lived to tell the tale.

There were other crashes. Every pilot survived. They were lucky. Early planes had no safety features. Not even seat belts. A chain drove the propeller. If it broke, it could snap **guy wires** or shred fabric.

The light machines were hard to handle. Many needed the weight of two people for balance. Some pilots used sandbags in place of the passenger. If a passenger shifted weight, the plane could go out of control.

In Reims, people talked about the "charmed lives" of fliers. It seemed so until the following year, when 32 **aviators** lost their lives. Most shared the feelings of Baroness Raymonde de Laroche, the world's first lady pilot. "It may be that I shall tempt Fate once too often. But it is to the air that I have dedicated myself, and I fly always without the slightest fear."

Yes, women had earned their wings. The young baroness was a French racing pilot. Blanche Scott, Bessica Raiche, Harriet Quimby, and Mathilde Moisant flew with the men on American exhibition teams.

By 1910, both Glenn Curtiss and the Wrights had opened flying schools. Their best pilots toured the country. They performed daring stunts. Female fliers climbing high, "death diving," and flipping upside down added color and thrills.

They all understood the danger of flying under bridges or bouncing their wheels along rooftops. So why did they do it?

Money drew many. In 1910, the average American made about $1,250 a year. Stunt pilots made between $1,000 and $5,000 per flight.

Harriet Quimby wanted to save enough to sit home and write books. In October 1910, the young journalist went to the Belmont Aviation Meet. In search of a story, she found a dream.

Claude Grahame-White

The final event was 33 miles. It ran from Belmont Park to the Statue of Liberty and back. The pilots took off one by one. They raced against the clock. By 3:30 p.m., Englishman Claude Grahame-White led with a time of 35 minutes, 21 seconds.

American John Moisant had wrecked his own plane. He borrowed another and lifted off a little past 4:00. Out across the harbor he flew, around the statue, and back again. The announcer read his time, "34 minutes, 47 seconds!" Moisant collected the $10,000 prize.

Harriet watched. She was amazed and delighted. Within months, she earned her pilot's

Harriet Quimby climbs into her Moisant monoplane.

license. She was the first American woman to do so. She went on to fly with the Moisant team.

In 1912, Harriet became the first woman to solo the English Channel. But she never got to write books. One day, she took a friend for a ride. A big gust of wind somersaulted the light plane. Pilot and passenger fell to their deaths.

Lincoln Beachey didn't care about money. The Curtiss School graduate flew for fame. As a boy, he was a chubby kid who was teased by classmates. But no one laughed once he took to the air.

Talented and fearless, Linc Beachey made his airplane do the impossible. He'd "seesaw" down a row of hangars, dipping a wing into each. He'd dive under bridges and power lines. He'd drop straight down. Crowds scattered as he leveled off just over their heads.

Beachey was the first American to loop-the-loop. And that was in a plane not built for stunt flying!

Lincoln Beachey flies under the Niagara Falls bridge.

In May 1911, Beachey rocketed down the Niagara River and over the falls. Honeymooners screamed as he vanished behind a white-water curtain. Seconds ticked by. Then out he flew. He was wet but all in one piece. Who needed barrels? Linc Beachey had taken Niagara Falls in an airplane.

Some people called him the "Flying Fool." Others agreed with Orville Wright who thought him "the greatest aviator of them all." Either way, no pilot could outdo him. Those who tried sometimes died.

One day a reporter shoved a paper in Beachey's face. "What about this?" he asked.

Linc read, "Rutherford Page . . . yesterday crashed to his death in Los Angeles after boasting that he would 'show Beachey a thing or two . . .' "

The flier stormed to his plane, started the engine, and climbed. At 11,575 feet, he ran out of gas. Down he came, fighting to land with a dead stick. Safely on the ground, he yelled, "I'm through with flying! I just set a new altitude record. And there's not a man alive I can't outfly. But I'll not take the blame for the carelessness of others!"

Had the great Linc Beachey folded his wings? Not for long. Flying was his life. He put on his thinking cap. Twenty-two men had died trying to copy his tricks. Why? All the accident reports said the same thing. The airplanes' engines had quit. They spiraled to earth and crashed.

Beachey had an idea. He took his airplane to 5,000 feet and switched off the motor. The plane jerked and fell, twisting.

Instinct told Linc to pull back on the wheel. To lift the nose. Surely that's what the others had done. So instead, he pushed forward. He steered hard against the spin. The force of the wind started the engine and the aircraft rolled level.

The Flying Fool had solved the stall-spin puzzle. It was his greatest gift to aviation.

Flying Circuses

Washington, D.C., went on full alert on September 28, 1914. People were nervous anyway. Across the Atlantic, World War I (WWI) had raged for over a month. America had not yet entered the conflict. But it seemed to be only a matter of time. So think how President Woodrow Wilson felt that sizzling afternoon.

Zzzzzzzzz! The rumble grew closer. President Wilson looked out the window. An airplane came zooming right at him. Would it crash into the White House? At the last second, the biplane climbed. Big block letters on the bottom wing read BEACHEY.

Woodrow Wilson

The president went outside to watch the aerobatic show. Congress called it a day and joined him. But just in case, the Secret Service drew their guns.

Beachey landed on the lawn of the Capitol building. Officials rushed him as he warned, "This is what can happen . . . with [a weak] air corps. America needs more planes."

Europe had been busy building warplanes for years. By the beginning of WWI, Germany had 1,200 combat planes. France and England each had 1,000. The United States had fewer than 20.

Any fool could see the army needed more. The Flying Fool had been trying to convince them since 1912. He wanted to teach their pilots too. But the military saw no need for daredevil flying. At least, not at first.

Early in the war, pilots simply observed enemy movements. Their slow, stable airplanes carried cameras, not weapons.

Flying Officers, Love Field Aviation Camp, Dallas, Texas, May 1918

Then someone figured a way to fire a machine gun through a spinning propeller. Hitting targets required faster flight and tighter turns. A new breed of aircraft appeared—the fighter.

These planes topped 125 mph. They could climb, dive, and turn in the blink of an eye. They needed pilots with quick thinking, quicker reflexes, and a lot of heart. They needed pilots like Linc Beachey or Frank Luke, "the balloon buster from Arizona."

Frank Luke, 1918

Some fliers didn't like Luke. They thought he bragged too much about shooting down dirigibles. But everyone respected his bravery.

America's "top gun" flew like a crazy man. Weaving in and out of German patrols, Luke shot down 18 enemy aircraft in 17 days. Five of his planes came back so full of holes they never flew again.

One day, Luke was grounded for not following orders. He took off anyway. As he did, he promised to destroy three German balloons. He kept his word.

Under heavy fire—*tat, tat, tat*—down went the first. On to the second. Then Luke took a bullet himself. Though badly hurt, he sent the third down in flames too. Still he kept on shooting at German troops on the ground.

WWI German fighter

Finally, Luke was forced down behind enemy lines. He fought with his pistol until he was killed by rifle fire.

Student pilots train with Jennys at Kelly Field in San Antonio, Texas, during WWI.

Orders or no, Frank Luke was awarded the Medal of Honor.

Aces like Luke helped the Allies win WWI. Afterward, those who lived had a choice. Most picked other lines of work. But many could do nothing but fly. Some found **sponsors**. Today, a sports star's picture on the box helps sell Wheaties. In the 1920s, a war hero's face helped sell everything from cigarettes to motor oil.

Airplanes were now faster, sturdier, and more dependable. Enclosed cabins carried more passengers. People could fly clear across continents. But most were afraid to try.

Manufacturers knew their aircraft were safer. As they searched for ways to prove it, a term popped up—**airmindedness**.

A lady in the sky made it seem friendlier. Soon every top female flier had a job pushing airmindedness. Women in goggles and leather helmets smiled from magazine covers. Inside were articles like "Shall You Let Your Daughter Fly?" In 1922, a girl was even boxed up and flown across the country as an airmail package.

Many fliers joined **flying circuses**. They carried airmindedness to small-town America. These **barnstormers** entertained country folk with colorful aerobatics. And for $1, anyone could take a ride. And what a ride it was for a farmer's son or rancher's daughter!

31

The Curtiss JN-4 was nicknamed "the Jenny." It was the most important American plane used during WWI. It was a trainer that was used to teach pilots to fly. It was well-built, but it had faults. It didn't have enough power, and it performed poorly. Better planes were developed so that by the end of the war, the Jenny was outdated.

The cheap postwar price of the Jennys made them popular for barnstorming. As a result, they were flown well into the 1930s.

One or two at a time, they'd climb into the open cockpit. The motor would roar to life. Down the runway they'd speed, breathing hot-oil smoke. Then the ground gave way to the freedom of the sky. They were flying!

The dollar-a-ride idea started with the Gates Flying Circus. Ivan Gates didn't fly himself. But he knew how to put on a show. He hired the very best pilots and parachutists.

When audiences tired of the same old routines, he looked for new amusements. Wing walking, the latest craze, looked exciting. But who would do such a thing? Time would tell.

Meanwhile, barnstormer Earl Dougherty had claimed he'd do the impossible. He would stay in the air for 24 hours!

Everyone knew his **Jenny** couldn't stay in the air 24 hours. It couldn't carry enough fuel. What trick did he have up his sleeve? Thousands showed up to find out.

After several hours, a second airplane buzzed into view. A daredevil named Wesley May knelt on the upper wing. On his back was a five-gallon gas

can. The plane pulled close to the Jenny. May stood, grabbed hold, and hauled himself aboard. Then he strolled down the wing and filled the Jenny's gas tank. Gates signed him on the spot.

May created more daring tricks. He would bicycle along the top wing or roller skate right off it.

Ruth Law Oliver

Others tried to top him. Ruth Law Oliver used ladders to climb from cars to airplanes or change planes in midair. "I was earning $9,000 a week at one point," she later said. "Imagine $9,000 a week in 1920!"

Only the best barnstormers made that kind of money. For some, maintenance and fuel ate up what little they earned. Others lost their lives trying. Especially before laws were passed to limit low-level flying. Wesley May was killed performing one of his stunts. He slipped off a

wing and fell into a cemetery. He died when his head hit a tombstone.

Flying circuses had clowns too. Wild Bill Kopia would dress up as a lady opera star and buy a ticket for a joyride. The announcer made a big deal about the "star" as "she" climbed into an idling Jenny. The pilot jumped out and ran back to the hangar for something he "forgot." Then while waving at the crowd, the opera star "accidentally" hit the gas.

The Jenny jumped forward, toward the grandstands. People screamed and shouted as the plane spun around. Down the field it went, carrying its "helpless" passenger toward a fence. Suddenly, the Jenny popped into the air and Kopia went into his aerobatic routine. Audiences loved it.

WWI pilot Doug Davis led a large crew of topflight barnstormers. The Doug Davis Flying Circus packed 'em in with the latest, greatest stunts. Then one day, no one showed up. Mabel Cody's Flying Circus had also come to town.

Sam Cody's niece was beautiful and bold. She would leap aboard a plane from a racing speedboat. She would wing-walk while her pilot rocked and rolled. And could she fly! In addition

Mabel Cody jumps from a speedboat to a plane in 1926.

to all that, she was just plain smart. Dozens of aerobats asked to join up with her. Mabel chose only the best.

Before each show, Mabel picked a "star." That pilot would outfly all the others. Crowds loved to watch the "ace" outdo the rest. Afterward, they'd line up around the block to fly with their hero and get his autograph.

Doug Davis had to do something. First, he tried to steal Mabel's best. He went after stars like Bonnie Rowe who hung beneath airplanes by the toes. Not even offering to double their paychecks would make them come over. So Davis tried a billboard blitz. But Mabel beat him to the towns where he put up his signs.

The only thing left was better tricks. The two outfits went head-to-head. The stunts they did got crazier and crazier. Before long, both crashed planes and lost pilots.

One day Davis extended an invitation to Mabel. "What do you say we join forces?"

Mabel's pilots agreed. But she had one condition. "Okay . . . but come up and fight first."

Davis's crew followed him up in the air where Mabel's team waited. Together they put on an amazing show. Then Mabel and Davis climbed. The other pilots pulled back to watch their bosses dive straight at each other. At the last second, they turned sideways, almost bumping wing tips.

Mabel came around behind Davis, matching his every loop and roll. He tried to shake her, flying sideways between rows of tall trees. She stayed on his tail. He flew under a bridge, upside down. She did the same. Finally, he saw a freight train. No way she'd do this!

Davis swung around, dropping over the train and slowing to match its speed. Plunk! He landed on top of a boxcar. Sure he'd proven himself the best pilot, Davis climbed from the cockpit. Then he looked over his shoulder.

On the car behind him, Mabel stood in front of her plane. "Okay, cowboy. Now how do you propose we get these things off here?"

The Doug Davis-Baby Ruth Flying Circus became the most famous barnstorming troupe in history.

Chapter 6

Derbies and Pylons

Aviation took a giant leap forward during the 1920s. The air devils had shown the world. Airplanes were here to stay! The pilots had taken flight to the masses and thrilled them with aerobatics. Now they wanted respect.

During the Golden Age of Aviation (1929–1939), they earned just that. Distance derbies and pylon racing tested courage and skill. America's National Air Races became aviation's proving ground.

In 1927, a young airmail pilot captured the world's attention. At 24, Charles Lindbergh had already logged 2,000 air hours. He'd barnstormed, wing-walked, and parachuted. But could he fly across the Atlantic from New York to Paris?

A $25,000 prize awaited the first person to make the 3,300-mile crossing.

Charles Lindbergh, May 21, 1927

Several attempts had failed. Those failures were mostly due to fierce Atlantic storms. Few of those planes were ever seen again.

Lindbergh found sponsors to build him a special airplane. It was powered by the new Wright Whirlwind engine. On May 20, 1927, the *Spirit of St. Louis* lifted off from New York. It vanished into a thick, gray mist.

The weather reports looked favorable. The plane was running fine. Lindbergh had figured his headings perfectly. He'd only forgotten one thing. When would he sleep?

Things really got bad when night fell. Lindbergh stomped his feet and bounced in his seat. He put his hands out the window into icy air. When all else failed, he held his eyelids open with his thumbs.

Lindbergh and monoplane designer Louis Bleriot, 1927

At daybreak, he dropped low over the ocean. Dazed but determined, he pushed on. After 26 hours, he saw birds. Then he saw boats. And finally, he saw land! He'd made it!

Lindberg's success inspired others. Within six weeks, two more planes had crossed the Atlantic. Another had flown across the Pacific.

The Oakland-Honolulu flight made big headlines. Army pilots Lester Maitland and Albert Hegenberger

Albert Hegenberger (left) and Lester Maitland (right)

couldn't make any mistakes. If they missed the Hawaiian Islands, they'd have to put down at sea. Rescue was unlikely. Imagine their relief when they spotted the tiny landforms surrounded by crashing surf.

That spurred the first **transoceanic** air race in August 1927. The Dole "Pineapple Derby" drew 16 entrants. Most were clueless. Two crashed before the race started. A quick inspection disqualified six more. Four either crashed on takeoff or turned back. Two finished the race. The other two disappeared.

Still, people now believed in the future of flight. In 1928, the number of licensed pilots tripled. Airlines carried four times more passengers than the year before. Airplane-manufacturing stocks boomed.

That money created state-of-the-art aircraft. Designers fashioned sleek machines. Mechanics built powerful engines capable of

great speeds. WWI planes could do 160 mph. In 1934, an Italian seaplane hit 441 mph. This **hydroplane** record stands today.

Air racing tested the courage of pilots and planes. Early events like the Pulitzer Prize Race (1920–1925) and Schneider Trophy (1913–1931) were mostly won by military fliers. In 1929, a California automobile dealer set out to change that.

Jimmy Doolittle and the biplane that won both the 1925 Pulitzer Prize Race (with wheels) and the 1925 Schneider Trophy (with pontoons)

Cliff Henderson was a slick salesman who offered every car buyer an airplane ride in one of his three Jennys. He kept them at Clover Field near Santa Monica, California.

In 1924, the army asked Henderson to welcome its round-the-world flying team. His efforts drew 200,000 people.

1924 Round-the-World flight crew

Navy Sea Hawks perform at the 1928 National Air Races.

Afterward, Henderson knew what he really wanted to do—promote air meets.

In 1928, he organized the National Air Races in a barley field that would later become the Los Angeles airport. People came from all over to watch aviation's brightest stars.

An autogiro is a rotary-wing aircraft that uses a propeller for forward motion and a freely rotating rotor for lift.

With his success, Henderson was invited to run the 1929 races in Cleveland. He decided to make it the most spectacular event in aviation history. Some of his ideas were so daring they were considered radical.

There were 35 **closed-course races**. Every type of aircraft raced, including gliders, balloons, and even an **autogiro**.

For the first time, some events used the "racehorse" start. Rather than taking off one at a time, planes lined up 50 feet apart and lifted off together. Cross-country events started from points all across the United States. They ended on the racing field.

The Women's Air Derby highlighted female fliers. The race would have challenged any pilot. The contestants needed 100 hours solo time with 25 hours in cross-country flights of 40 miles or more. Forty American women qualified. Eighteen entered including Amelia Earhart. She would later become the first woman to solo the Atlantic in 1932. Joining the Americans were German Thea Rasche and Australian Jessie Miller.

The "Petticoat Pilots," as the press called them, began the eight-day **marathon** in Santa Monica. The women flew between dawn and dusk. They covered about 300 miles each day, even with stops for rest and fuel.

These women used road maps and compasses to make their way across the shifting landscape. For emergencies, they carried a parachute, one gallon of water, a three-day supply of beef jerky, and malted milk tablets.

At first, dust clouds, drifting sand, and heat haze made it hard to find landing strips. Later, driving rainstorms had the same effect. The pilots kept their cool despite danger above and below.

Over western Texas, Blanche Noyes noticed flames. She landed quickly. But she lost a tire in the thick brush. Blanche put out the blaze with handfuls of sand. Then she took off and finished the race with the damaged wheel.

Amelia Earhart, Ruth Nichols, and Louise Thaden

Others blew off course, ran out of fuel, or lost engines. Bobbi Trout cartwheeled during an emergency landing. She climbed from her ruined plane without a scratch. Hollywood stunt flier Pancho Barnes clipped a car and also walked away.

Margaret Perry flew with a high fever for two days until typhoid forced her to quit. Distance flier Ruth Nichols led until the last day. The wind pushed her into a tractor and out of the race.

Cross-country flier Marvel Crosson bailed out when her engine quit. She was too low for her parachute to open completely. Marvel died when she hit the ground. She was wrapped in brightly colored silk.

Ruth Nichols

Amelia Earhart (left) with Florence Klingensmith (right). Klingensmith was the only female flier registered in the 1933 Phillips Trophy Race in Chicago. She was killed when she had to bail out of her damaged Gee Bee Model Y plane. She was too close to the ground for her parachute to open completely.

In men's racing, such mishaps were considered part of the game. But female racers faced headlines like

WOMEN HAVE CONCLUSIVELY PROVEN THAT THEY CANNOT FLY

Texas oil man J. D. Halliburton called for a halt to the race. "Women have been dependent on men for so long that . . . they are handicapped. Stop the race. For the sake of the women."

Event manager Frank Copeland answered, "There will be no stopping this race!"

Louise Thaden

Women everywhere cheered as 15 racers crossed the finish line. They were led by Louise Thaden. Afterward, no one could deny their skills as topflight pilots.

The finale of the '29 Nationals was a 50-mile pylon race. Two **civilian** racers would take on the military's two best planes. Both the army and navy Curtiss Hawks had been streamlined and souped up. Most people figured one of them would win although the civilian Lockheed Vega had finished well the year before. The second nonmilitary entry was top secret. So secret, in fact, its name was *Mystery.*

On takeoff, Doug Davis in *Mystery* grabbed the lead. But the flying-circus ace cut a pylon and had to turn back to circle it. A mile behind the army Hawk, Davis gunned his mystery ship. One newspaper wrote that the propeller sang "like a siren" as the plane closed the gap.

Mystery took the checkered flag. Next came the army plane, the Vega, and the navy Hawk. Civilian planes had bested military might. And they continued to do so for many years.

Most planes were built by small companies with good ideas. Monoplanes replaced biplanes. Light metals replaced wood. Lightweight engines replaced heavier models. The most daring designs were very fast. They were also quite dangerous!

The Gee Bee racers topped that list from 1931 through 1935. Built by the Granville brothers, these tiny planes reached wicked speeds. But they were tricky.

Gee Bee Model Z Super Sportster (top)
Gee Bee Model Y Senior Sportster (bottom)

Racing pilot Jimmy Haizlip took one flight in a Gee Bee Model Z. Afterward, he said, "My first shock came when I touched the rudder. The thing tried to bite its own tail."

Jimmy Doolittle called the Gee Bee R-1 the touchiest plane he'd ever been in. On his first practice run, he climbed to 5,000 feet to try some pylon turns. (Racing altitude is 250 feet or lower.)

Doolittle later said, "That airplane did two snap rolls before I could get it under control. Had I practiced that near the ground I would have been dead." Soon, however, he and his Gee Bee set a new world speed record of 309 mph.

In 1930, Cliff Henderson introduced a new closed-course event, the Thompson Trophy. The Bendix Cross-Country Race was added in 1931. Every racing pilot wanted to win the Thompson or the Bendix Trophy. The two became the yardstick measuring pilot skill and aircraft excellence. That lured spectators by the thousands.

Jimmy Doolittle

For many during the 1930s, Labor Day weekend was National Air Race weekend. People would save all year to vacation at Henderson's thrilling show. There they watched greats like Jimmy Doolittle and Roscoe Turner, neck and neck in Gee Bee and Wedell-Williams racers. Fighting for the title, they flew low over the field. The extreme risk factor only added excitement.

Both pilots had won the Bendix. So had Doug Davis and Jimmy Haizlip. In 1936, Louise Thaden stunned the air-racing scene. She became the first woman to win the trophy. Two years later, Jacqueline Cochran repeated the feat.

Some of the decade's best fliers never won either race. Yet pilots like Howard Hughes continued to set speed marks. Seaplanes held the record until 1939. It then fell to German land planes as that country once again prepared for war.

Roscoe Turner and his Wedell-Williams racer

Chapter 7

War Birds and Dogfights

In March 1939, Adolf Hitler invaded Czechoslovakia. Francisco Franco took control of Spain. The next month, Italy captured Albania. On September 1, Hitler sent his **panzer** tank

Hitler (left) and Franco (right)

divisions rolling into Poland. Two days later, France and England declared war against Germany. World War II (WWII) had begun. History's most destructive conflict would last until 1945.

On one side stood the Axis Powers—Germany, Italy, and Japan. On the other, the Allies—Great Britain, France, the Soviet Union, China, and the United States.

Blitzkrieg damage in London

WWII blazed across Europe. This was a different kind of war from any before.

Hitler's ground troops overran the continent. They were aided by the **blitzkrieg**. It quickly became clear that air power would help decide victory. Worldwide, the call went out for pilots.

America stayed out of the conflict as long as possible. But that changed on December 7, 1941. That morning, 23-year-old flight instructor Cornelia Fort took a student up to practice **touch-and-gos**. As they turned to land, an airplane came right at them.

Cornelia recalled, "I jerked the controls away . . . and jammed the throttle wide open to pull above the oncoming plane. As it passed underneath, I saw red balls on the wings shining in the sun. We were familiar with the emblem of the Rising Sun on passenger ships but not on military planes. I looked toward Pearl Harbor and saw billowing black smoke . . ."

The Japanese attack took America—and the world—by complete surprise. Bombs rained from the sky. Flames swallowed ships and planes as American soldiers jumped from Sunday morning slumber.

Cornelia couldn't believe her eyes. "I knew the air was not the place for my little airplane. I landed quickly. A few seconds later, a shadow passed over me, spattering bullets."

The next day, the United States and England declared war on Japan. Germany then declared war on the United States. Though angry, America was not prepared to fight in both Asia and Europe. The Army Air Force had only 1,100 combat-ready planes. Most were old and slow, no match for Japanese Zeros or German Messerschmitts. America needed new aircraft and trained pilots to fly them.

Factories fired up 24 hours a day. Women had to run them because their men had marched off to war. The female workforce doubled. And they did a fine job.

Over the next four years, the American aircraft industry turned out 300,000 military aircraft. But with most male pilots flying combat missions, who would deliver them to airfields? Who would fly supplies and train new pilots?

The Women Airforce Service Pilots (WASPS) did much of that work. Led by Nancy Love and Jacqueline Cochran, the WASPS ferried planes, taught cadets, tested new aircraft, and towed targets for gunnery practice. The last was by far their most dangerous job.

Cruising at 10,000 feet, the pilot pulled a fabric sleeve for inexperienced soldiers to shoot at. Many planes returned to base with bullet holes in their tail.

The WASPS flew 12,650 planes (77 different types) a total of 60 million miles. During this time 76 died—38 in accidents, 11 in training, and 27 during operations. Among them was Cornelia Fort. She was the first American woman to die flying for her country.

America's best male fliers also answered the call to arms. Jimmy Doolittle took command of 16 B-25 bombers. On April 18, 1942, Doolittle and his men lifted off from the carrier *Hornet*. They roared over Tokyo and nearby cities, hitting their targets. But they didn't have enough fuel to return to friendly airfields. One plane reached Russia. Crews ditched the planes behind enemy lines. Most of the men, including Doolittle, finally found their way home.

B-25 on the Doolittle raid takes off from the *USS Hornet*.

Charles Lindbergh flew the gleaming new Corsair FG-1. It was beautiful, fast, and deadly. As he later wrote in the *Saturday Evening Post*, "Sixteen hundred rounds I carry, of .50-calibre ammunition . . . Suddenly the grace of flight is gone. I see with war-conditioned eyes—these are wicked-looking planes we fly, manned by ruthless pilots . . ."

Boyington's Black Sheep Squadron

The first 400-mph military plane, the Corsair replaced aging F4F Wildcats. Wildcats were tough but no match for Zeros in a tight dogfight. Pilot Greg "Pappy" Boyington called the Corsair a sweet flying baby. "It could climb with a Zero . . . and had considerably more speed. With the Corsair, we could make our own rules."

XF4U-1 Corsair

Midway through the war, other new aircraft came on the scene. P-51 Mustangs could fly 850 miles without refueling. This let them go deep into enemy territory. Built for quick

P-51 Mustang Group pilots

takeoffs from carrier decks, F8F Bearcats became the navy's top fighters. The P-38 Lightning's unusual design made it a difficult target. P-38s often escorted bombers on raids.

Pilots with an F6F fighter on the *USS Lexington* in 1943

As these planes appeared, the tide turned in favor of the Allies.

P-38-L

Liberator bomber flies over P-40 fighter planes in 1943.

By May 1945, heavy Allied bombing had toppled Germany. Fighting in the Pacific continued as Japan refused to give up. But America had a secret—and terrible—weapon.

Early on August 6, the B-29 *Enola Gay* opened her bomb-bay doors. The world's first atomic bomb destroyed Hiroshima. Two days later, the B-29 *Bock's Car* dropped another. A mushroom cloud swallowed Nagasaki. With the dawn of the nuclear age, Japan at last surrendered. WWII was over.

The 1946 National Air Races returned to Cleveland. But the country had tired of dogfights. Most of the racers were **war birds**, reminders of a time people wanted to forget.

For three years, interest in the event built slowly. Then in 1949, an inexperienced pilot missed a pylon, overcorrected, and flipped. He crashed into a house, killing the family inside. The city of Cleveland had had enough. Pilots hangared their racers. They put Bearcats and Mustangs to bed.

Fifteen years later, a Nevada rancher and hydroplane racer decided to awaken the sleeping speedsters. Bill Stead had read about them as a boy. Now he wanted to see them in action. 1964 was Nevada's 100th anniversary of statehood. With the help of Governor Grant Sawyer, Bill Stead made the National Air Races a part of Nevada's **centennial** celebration.

Closed-course pylon racing found a new home near Reno at Stead, Nevada.

TBF Avengers (navy torpedo planes)

Rare Bear

Chapter

Sky Racers

In 1964, around 40,000 flight lovers watched Bill Stead's own Bearcat take the unlimited **gold**. Now, over 200,000 people attend the Reno National Championship Air Races every year. Once again, it's *the* place to be in September. Bearcats, Mustangs, and Sea Furies once again take to the air to do battle in the unlimited class.

Every part of their motors is brand-new. This makes them even faster. With clipped wings and lowered canopies, they can turn even tighter.

Such **modifications** bother aviation lovers who would rather see war birds **restored**. They may have a point. Of 850 Bearcats built, only a few remain. Lyle Shelton's *Rare Bear* has a motor from a B-29. Whether that's right or wrong, *Rare Bear* holds the world record of 529 mph.

Unlimited pilot Bill (Tiger) Destefani races a highly modified P-51. His *Strega* regularly challenges *Rare Bear* in the championship showdown. Tiger admits *Strega* isn't really a war bird anymore. "It's a racer. It's got its own identity."

Homebuilt unlimiteds seem like the answer, but they haven't met with success. The two most promising, the ultramodern *Pond Racer* and the P-51 look-alike *Tsunami*, were lost in accidents. Yet as war birds retire, homebuilts may be the only way for unlimited air racing to continue.

Other WWII aircraft race in separate classes. Both the T-6s and T-28s were trainers. In them, rookie pilots learned to climb, dive, loop, and otherwise outfly the enemy. The trainers top out about 240 mph and can't beat the unlimiteds. But they're still exciting to watch.

When it comes to speed, design means more than size. The baby biplanes are the slowest. As air pushes against their boxy shape, it increases **drag**.

T-6 "Warlock"

The tiny formula ones run faster than the big trainers. These experimental planes are very small. Many pilots build them in

their garages at home. A formula one's sleek, angled shape cuts through the air. Think of brightly painted bullets whizzing across the sky.

Patti Johnson races both. Her biplane usually takes the gold. But she'd rather fly her formula. "Serious air racing is a lot of work,"

Biplane

Formula one "Nemesis"

she said. "Being the fastest plane in the field and constantly after record speed takes real concentration. My biplane is difficult to fly. The formula one is a joy. It would be lucky to win the **bronze**, so I can relax and have fun."

Jon Sharp's beautiful little *Nemesis* holds the formula one record. Modeled by a computer and made of **graphite**, Nemesis has topped 260 mph. It's the fastest four-cylinder machine in the world. No wonder so many fans think this is the most exciting class. The new sport class (kit-built planes) promises similar excitement.

The top prize is $60,000. That sounds like a lot of money. But it's only half the cost of a blown

Formula one "Miss USA"

engine. Figure in travel, entry fees, and mechanics' salaries and you'll see air racing is not about big bucks. It's about big egos and searching for big fun.

Most racers do fly for a living. They captain airlines, dust crops, or perform aerobatic routines. Many flew in WWII, Korea, Vietnam, or Desert Storm. For all, air racing is an exciting weekend game.

All pilots play to win. But they always play by the rules.

- Little planes use the racehorse start. Big ones take off one at a time. Then they line up for an airborne "go." Either way, no one jumps the gun.

- Races run counterclockwise.

- Pilots must stay above the top of the pylons but lower than 1,500 feet.

- Slower planes must let faster ones pass. Interfering could spell disaster.

Crashes happen. Pilots accept that risk. If they survive an accident, they learn from it. Unlimited pilot David Price went down his rookie year. "That didn't make me go slower," he said. "It made me train better." Now he takes home the gold.

Okay, ready for some fun? You've met the pilots, know the rules, and understand the danger. You've watched a race. Now fly one.

Come on! Taste the thrill! Climb into the cockpit of an unlimited racer.

Start your Rolls Royce engine. Listen to its perfectly tuned growl. Signal "ready" and your crew removes the wheel blocks.

Your feet are against the pedals. Your hands hold the wheel. You taxi down the runway and wait for the Bearcat in front of you to lift off. It's in the air. Your turn.

Gun your engine. Gather speed. Faster! Faster! You're off the ground.

It's hot and windy today. The race will be fast and bumpy. You give your seat belt an extra tug and fall in behind the pace plane. Once everyone lines up straight, your radio crackles, "Ladies and gentlemen, you have a race!"

Imagine wingtip-to-wingtip flight. Rivals are all around you. The slightest move means danger. But you have to move to win.

Up high, the air is smooth. You can't turn close around the pylons. That costs precious seconds. Too low, and swift desert updrafts toss you around like a balsa-wood model.

You can't let the plane in front get too far ahead. But you can't ride his tail either. **Prop wash** makes your war bird dance.

Give it all you've got on the straightaways. Slow down for the pylons. Here comes one now! Swing wide, lose time. But don't cut the corner!

A judge on the ground at each pylon makes sure nobody cheats.

Focus. Never give less than your best.

The other pilots trust you to race fast but fly safe. In fact, they expect perfection. Your little mistake could make someone else crash. That could result in loss of plane or life.

The racing circle stays small. If you hotdog or take too many chances, you're out of the game for good.

Another plane passes, spitting smoke in your face. Smell that hot oil? Faster! Your P-51 shudders and screams with effort. You ask for more. You believe the plane can handle it and pass the one in front. Sometimes it happens that way.

Sometimes the motor blows and forces a life-or-death emergency landing. But you have to take the chance. Risk is part of the game. Today Lady Luck smiles.

There's the white flag. Last lap and you're five seconds behind. It's all or nothing. Go for the gold! Pull back on the stick. Feel the force of your war bird's climb. Now, push hard. Let the plane dive.

Your stomach drops at the 500-mph rush. You've got the leader! You cross the finish line. You're ahead by the nose of a P-51. The crowd goes wild. This time they're cheering for you.

That's air racing—excitement, skill, and the courage to push the envelope until the checkered flag. Hope to see you there.

Until then, as the air devils say, "Fly low, fly fast, turn left."

Glossary

aerial	of, relating to, or occurring in the air
aerobatics	spectacular flying feats and maneuvers
aeronaut	one who travels or operates in an airship or balloon
aeroplane	early spelling of *airplane*
airmindedness	interest in air travel
airspace	space lying above a nation and coming under its control
altitude	height above a surface
ascend	to move upward
autogiro	rotary-wing aircraft that uses a propeller for forward motion and freely rotating rotor for lift
aviator	operator or pilot of an aircraft
barnstormer	pilot who traveled through rural districts performing aerial stunts
biplane	aircraft with two wings—one above the body and one below
blitzkrieg	violent surprise attack by massed air and ground forces
bronze	third-place prize
centennial	100th anniversary or its celebration
civilian	person not in the military
closed-course race	race around pylons

crop duster	person who sprays crops with fungicides or insecticides from an airplane; airplane used for spraying
Daedalus and Icarus	characters from Greek mythology. They made wings of wax and feathers to escape imprisonment on Crete. Icarus fell to the sea and drowned when he flew too close to the sun and the wax melted.
Dark Ages	from about 400 A.D. to about 1000 A.D.; period during which civilization underwent a decline
descent	downward movement
dirigible	powered balloon
drag	force that causes something to slow down
emporium	commercial center
flying circus	group of barnstormers, skydivers, and pilots who entertained crowds with aerial acts
gold	first-place prize
gondola	pilot/passenger space below an airship
graphite	material made from carbon
guy wire	brace, guide, or support
heat	preliminary contests or races to narrow the competition
hydrogen	gas that is lighter than air; highly flammable
hydroplane	powerboat designed for racing that skims the surface of water; seaplane
inflate	to expand with air

the Jenny	nickname given to the Curtiss JN-4; used as a trainer during WWI and for barnstorming after the war
jet stream	long, narrow current of high-speed, high-altitude winds that generally blows from the west at speeds of 250 mph or more
lift	force that works against the pull of gravity
maneuver	to make a series of changes in direction and position
marathon	long-distance race
modification	change made to the original
monoplane	aircraft with one wing
ornithopter	aircraft designed to get its main support and power from flapping wings

Gee Bee

panzer	German WWII tank
prop wash	tricky wind currents caused by a propeller
pylon	a post or tower marking a prescribed course of an airplane's flight
restored	put back in the original state
spirit	flammable liquid
sponsor	a person or organization that pays for someone's project or activities
stratosphere	part of the earth's atmosphere that extends from about 7 miles above the surface to about 31 miles
supersonic	from one to five times the speed of sound in the air
superstition	idea maintained despite evidence to the contrary
tether	to hold an object in place with a rope or chain so that it can only move a certain distance
touch-and-go	practice landing and takeoff in an airplane. The plane makes a landing but immediately accelerates to take off again.
transoceanic	crossing the ocean
tribe	social group made up of numerous families
unlimited	the biggest, fastest piston-powered racing plane
war bird	plane that had been used for war

Index